...atinos ✳

...PE
FRANCIS

The People's Pope

Richard Worth

Enslow Publishing
101 W. 23rd Street
Suite 240
New York, NY 10011
USA
enslow.com

Published in 2016 by Enslow Publishing, LLC
101 W. 23rd Street, Suite 240, New York, NY 10011

Library of Congress Cataloging-in-Publication Data
Worth, Richard, author.
Pope Francis: the people's pope/Richard Worth.
 pages cm.—(Influential Latinos)
Includes bibliographical references and index.
Summary: "Describes the life, tribulations, and achievements of Pope Francis"—Provided by publisher.
Audience: Ages 12-up.
ISBN 978-0-7660-7328-9
1. Francis, Pope, 1936——Juvenile literature. 2. Popes—Biography—Juvenile literature. 3. Catholic Church—Clergy—Biography—Juvenile literature. 4. Papacy—History—Juvenile literature. I. Title.
BX1378.7.W67 2016
282.092—dc23
[B]
                          2015027524
Printed in the United States of America

To Our Readers: We have done our best to make sure all website addresses in this book were active and appropriate when we went to press. However, the author and the publisher have no control over and assume no liability for the material available on those websites or on any websites they may link to. Any comments or suggestions can be sent by e-mail to customerservice@enslow.com.

Photo Credits: Cover, p. 1 Franco Origlia/Getty Images news/Getty Images; p. 4 Franco Origlia/ Getty Images News/Getty Images; p. 8 Christopher Furlong/Getty Images News/Getty Images; p. 11 Filippo Monteforte/AFP/Getty Images; p. 15 ullstein bild/ullstein bild via Getty Images; p. 17 API/GAMMA/Gamma-Rapho via Getty Images; p. 20 Jesuit General Curia via Getty Images News/ Getty Images; p. 25 Grupo44/LatinContent WO/Getty Image; p. 28 Grupo44/LatinContent WO/ Getty Images; p. 30 Paul Schutzer/The LIFE Picture Collection/Getty Images; p. 32 Jesuit General Curia/Getty Images News/Getty Images; p. 35 Jesuit General Curia/Getty Images Europe/Getty Images; p. 39 Keystone-France/Gamma-Keystone via Getty Images; 42 Michael Brennan/Hulton Archive/Getty Images; p. 46 API/GAMMA/Gamma-Rapho via Getty Images; p. 49 Daniel Luna/ AFP/Getty Images; p. 54 Rafael Wollmann/Gamma-Rapho via Getty Images; p. 58 Associated Press; p. 63 Emiliano Lasalvia/LatinContent WO/Getty Images; p. 65 Grzegorz Galazka\Archivio Grzegorz Galazka\Mondadori Portfolio via Getty Images; p. 71 Raimundo Vinuelas/AFP/Getty Images; p. 74 Gianni Ferrari/Cover/ GettyImages; p. 77 Gary Payne/Liaison/Hulton Archive/Getty Images; p. 80 Juan Mabromata/AFP/Getty Images; p. 84 snapshot-photography/ullstein bild via Getty Images; p. 86 Grupo13/LatinContent Editorial/Getty Images; p. 91 Silvina Parma/MDQ Fotobank/LatinContent WO/Getty Images; 93 Maxi Failla/AFP/Getty Images; Cézaro De Luca/EPA/Newscom; p. 99 Associated Press; p. 101 © Stephen Bisgrove / Alamy Stock Photo; p. 104 Associated Press; p. 107 © RealyEasyStar/ Fotografia Felici / Alamy Stock Photo; p. 110 Ivan Romano/Getty Images News/ Getty Images; p. 112 Franco Origlia/Getty Images News/Getty Images.

Contents

Pope Benedict XVI surprised the world when he resigned from his position in 2013.

Chapter 1

ELECTION AS POPE

In February 2013, Pope Benedict XVI shocked the Catholic Church with an unexpected announcement in the Vatican—headquarters of the Church in Rome. As he stood before a group of cardinals—the leaders of the Church—Benedict announced, "I have come to the certainty that my strengths, due to an advanced age, are no longer suited to an adequate exercise of the Petrine mystery."[1] Benedict was resigning as the 265th Pope since St. Peter—the first pope, or head of the Church, in the first century CE.

Benedict's resignation was almost unheard of because most popes died while in office. Benedict was the first pope to resign in 600 years. But he was eighty-six years old, and his eight-year papacy had been marked by a variety of major problems. Among these was corruption at the highest levels of the Church, costing millions of euros (European currency). In addition, the Church had been involved with a scandal involving priests and nuns who had sexually abused little children.

Benedict had become pope in 2005, following the long papal rule of Pope John Paul II, which lasted twenty-seven years. Cardinal Joseph Ratzinger, as he was known before becoming Pope Benedict, was a close associate of John Paul and was considered the likely candidate to succeed him. For the election of a new pope, the cardinals assembled in Rome from across the world. They came from Europe, Africa, Latin America, and the United States.

One hundred and fifteen of them met in 2005 at what is known as a conclave in the Sistine Chapel at the Vatican to consider the candidates to become the next pope. While there were more than 115 cardinals in the Church, only those who were under 80 are permitted to vote in the conclave. A candidate for pope must receive at least 77 votes, a two-thirds majority, to be elected.

As the cardinals cast secret ballots for the next pope, the Catholic world awaited outside to find out their choice. If no pope received the necessary majority on a ballot, black smoke circled up through the chimney at the Vatican. White smoke, on the other hand, indicated that a new pope had been selected. The first three ballots did not end in the selection of a new pope. While Cardinal Ratzinger received 72 votes on the third ballot, it was five short of the number necessary for election.

Second in the voting, with 40, was a surprise candidate, Cardinal Jorge Mario Bergoglio, cardinal of Buenos

Aires, Argentina. Latin America has approximately 143 million Roman Catholics, out of 1.2 billion people worldwide. Bergoglio was known as a reformer, and many other cardinals believed that he would be a good choice. However, popes were traditionally Italian. John Paul, a Polish cardinal, had been an exception. And Ratzinger, a German cardinal, would also have been an exception. But no pope had ever been selected from Africa, Asia, or the Americas.

Finally on the fourth ballot, Cardinal Bergoglio asked his supporters to vote for Ratzinger. Outside, the assembled crowds saw white smoke drifting upward from the Vatican, indicating that a new pope had been elected.

A Transition Period

Because of his age when he became pope, seventy-eight, Ratzinger was considered a transitional pope who would have a short reign. But no one had ever guessed that he would resign before his death. His resignation in 2013 meant that the cardinals had to assemble in Rome once again for another election.

In Buenos Aires, Cardinal Bergoglio received a first class ticket from the Vatican for the long flight to Rome. A humble man, Bergoglio instead asked for a seat in coach but requested one with extra legroom because he is quite tall, over six feet. One of his assistants also collected money to buy the cardinal a new pair of shoes, to replace the old black ones that he usually wore.

The scene of white smoke swirling out of the Vatican chimney is a sign that the cardinals have selected a new pope.

Once in Rome, most cardinals traveled from the airport to the Vatican in limousines. But Bergoglio took the train and then a bus to a modest hotel where he had stayed in the past while visiting Rome. Bergoglio was not considered to be in the running to succeed Pope Benedict. Instead the favorites were Cardinal Angelo Scola of Milan, an Italian, and Cardinal Marc Ouellet, a Canadian, who had worked in the Vatican for many years.

These men were considered relatively conservative—that is, they believed that the Roman Curia, which administered the Church from Rome, should continue to have the power to run the Church. Regardless of the scandals that had rocked the Catholic Church in the last two decades, Scola and Ouellet were not expected to call for a sharing of power between the Curia and the cardinals throughout the rest of the world.

However, many of the cardinals who would select a new pope disagreed with this position. Cardinals from Latin America, the United States, and Europe believed it was time for a significant change. The Church, they believed, was losing its way and needed to be more responsive to the needs of its many members.

Some of these cardinals considered that Bergoglio might be a good choice. They knew him from the last conclave, had worked with him at other meetings, and recognized that he was a reformer. But it seemed unlikely that he could get enough votes to defeat the favorites. However, at a meeting of the cardinals before the conclave began, Bergoglio was among several speakers who addressed his colleagues: "The evils that, over time, appear in Church institutions have their root in [self-centeredness] . . . Jesus says he is at the door and calling . . . to be let in. But I sometimes think that Jesus is knocking from the inside, for us to let him out."[2]

Many of the cardinals in the room were strongly moved by Cardinal Bergoglio's statement. He seemed to promise a revitalization of the Church, moving it out from its center in the Vatican to the rest of the world, moving it away from a focus on wealth and the doctrines of the past to an embrace of the people—especially poor people everywhere.

The Conclave

On March 12, 2013, several days after this short speech, the cardinals met in their conclave to select a new pope. The reformers had decided to support Bergoglio, although Scola still seemed to be the favorite. As a result, those who supported him were surprised that Bergoglio received the most votes on the first ballot. By the third ballot, he had been elected the 216th pope of the Catholic Church and the first ever from Latin America. As one of his associates put it, Bergoglio was nervous about accepting such a high position, but he was surprisingly calm, believing it to be "the will of God."[3]

Bergoglio had received over 95 votes, far more than a two-thirds majority. As is the custom of a papal conclave, the new pope must be asked if he will accept his election. Cardinal Bergoglio agreed, adding "even though I am a great sinner."[4] This was a further signal of his humility. Then he must tell the other cardinals what name he wished to have as the new pope. To everyone's surprise, he chose Francis, after St. Francis of Assisi, a twelfth-century clergyman who gave up his wealth to work among the poor. It was another signal of the new pope's humility.

Afterward, he went out on the balcony of St. Peter's Church in the Vatican to see the assembled crowds in

Shortly after being elected, Jorge Mario Bergoglio, Pope Francis, appeared on the balcony of St. Peter's to greet the waiting crowds.

the huge square where a light rain was falling. Dressed in white, the new pope stood with some of the cardinals who had elected him. Instead of blessing the people in the square, as other popes had done, he asked for "the blessing of a people over its bishop—your prayer over me."[5] It was another signal that this pope would be quite different from many of those who had gone before him.

Chapter 2

ITALIAN ROOTS

Pope Francis had come home to Italy, the home of his ancestors. The pope's grandparents, Giovanni Angelo and Rosa Bergoglio, had spent much of their early married life in Asti, located in the north—the Piedmont region of Italy. In 1920, after their six children were born, the Bergoglios then moved about thirty miles to Turin, where the couple opened a small coffee shop. The family lived in Turin for the next seven years, but late in 1927 they embarked on the ship *Guilio Cesare* (*Julius Caesar*) for Argentina.

Angelo's brothers had already immigrated to Argentina in 1920. They they had set up a small road paving company in Parana, a port near the capital, Buenos Aires. They had been part of a huge European migration that had already brought 4.3 million immigrants to Argentina between 1890 and 1914. The Bergoglio paving company had done very well over the next seven years, enabling the brothers to build a large house called Palazzo Bergoglio. But a short time later, in 1930, the world was plunged into the Great Depression. The economy in Argentina declined, throwing thousands of people out of work, including the Bergoglios, who lost the paving business and their grand family home.

The Bergoglios left Parana and moved to the much larger city of Buenos Aires, hoping to find work. Mario, who was Giovanni's and Rosa's oldest son, had become very friendly with a local Italian priest, Father Enrico Pozzoli. When his parents moved to Buenos Aires, Father Pozzoli enabled them to borrow a small amount of money so they could once again open a small coffee shop—just as they had in Turin. Meanwhile, Mario, who had been trained as an accountant in Italy, succeeded in finding some work keeping the financial records of local businesses. This, combined with his parents' earnings, helped keep the family afloat during the worst of the economic crisis.

Mario was a devout Catholic who regularly attended the Catholic Church of St. Anthony of Padua near his home in Buenos Aires. There he met Maria Sivori Sturla in 1934, and the couple were married a year later in December 1935. Over the next few years, Maria gave birth to five children. The oldest, born in 1936, was Jorge Mario Bergoglio, the future Pope Francis.

Growing Up in Buenos Aires

For the next twenty years, Jorge lived at his parents' home at 531 Calle Membrillar in a working class neighborhood of Buenos Aires. There he was surrounded by family, Italian neighbors, and the influence of the Catholic Church. "My mother had my first brother when I was

Bergoglio grew up in Buenos Aires with his family, who had emigrated from Italy one generation earlier.

thirteen months old," Pope Francis once recalled. "[T]here are five of us in all. My grandparents lived around the corner, and, in order to help my mother, my grandmother would come and fetch me in the morning, take me to her house, and bring me back in the evening. My grandparents spoke Piedmontese to each other, and I picked it up from them."[1]

Jorge's grandmother, Rosa, instilled in him a devotion to the Catholic Church. She taught him his prayers from a very young age, took him to church, and explained some of the mysteries of Christianity. As a young woman back in Italy, Rosa had participated in a political group known as Catholic Action. She had delivered fiery speeches that criticized Italian dictator Benito Mussolini's government and its desire to control the Catholic Church. When the family left Italy in 1927, Rosa had been relieved to escape Mussolini's dictatorship.[2]

At the age of five, Jorge attended a kindergarten run by Catholic nuns. He became especially friendly with Sister Dolores Toledo, who later taught him the principles of the Catholic faith, found in the Catechism. Like Jorge's grandmother Rosa, Sister Dolores had a profound influence on his early life and his devout Christian faith. Most importantly, perhaps, she emphasized the responsibility that Christians have toward people who are poor and less fortunate.[3]

As he grew older, Jorge entered elementary school, where he played soccer and began to distinguish himself as an excellent student. Meanwhile, outside his classroom

The pope's parents, Maria and Mario Bergoglio, were devout Catholics who raised Jorge and his siblings with devotion, love, and warmth.

door, Argentina was undergoing a profound change. In 1946, General Juan Domingo Peron was elected president of the country. Peron was a champion of the poor and strongly supported the efforts of the Catholic Church to help them. Since the Catholic Church was one of the most powerful institutions in Argentina, Peron's alliance with the Church helped to solidify his power and popularity. Over the next few years, he began numerous programs designed to raise wages and expand the number of jobs for working class Argentinians.

While Argentina was in the midst of these enormous changes, Jorge's life was changing, too. His mother unexpectedly became partially paralyzed after her fifth child, Maria Elena, was born. She was unable to take care of her younger children without Rosa's help. And the other children, including Jorge, were sent away to boarding schools run by the Catholic Church.

Over the next few years, his love of learning and his faith were strengthened even further. "I learned, almost unconsciously, to seek the meaning of things," he recalled. At his school, the priests emphasized the importance of helping the poor, even if it meant giving up things for yourself.[4] After boarding school, Jorge began attending a vocational school, where he studied to become a chemical technician. He went to class in the morning and began working part time in the afternoons. His jobs included cleaning, secretarial work, and finally a position at a food laboratory. "I had an extraordinary boss there, Esther de Balestrino de Careaga . . .[who]

taught me the seriousness of hard work. . . . In particular in the laboratory I got to see the good and bad of human endeavor."[5]

Esther de Balestrino was a social activist and, during President Peron's first four-year term, many of the policies favored by such people became law. There were new laws controlling child labor—a problem that had

Evita

Eva Peron was one of the most remarkable leaders of the twentieth century. Born in 1919, she married Juan Domingo Peron in 1945, who was almost twenty-five years her senior. A beautiful actress and a gifted politician, she helped organize support for Peron that led to his first election as president in 1946. Once in office, Evita—as she was called—directed the health and labor departments in the new government.

In her emotional speeches, Evita passionately supported an expansion of women's rights, which led to their being given the right to vote, and advocated increased aid for the poor. These speeches attracted millions of Argentinians to her.

By the time Juan Peron won a second term, Evita was already dying of cancer, which claimed her life in 1952 when she was only thirty-three years old. In the aftermath of her death, Peron tried to turn his wife into a modern-day saint, but by then he was beginning to lose support among the Argentinian people.

As a boy, Jorge was sent away to a Catholic boarding school when his mother could no longer care for him.

been eliminated in the United States decades earlier—as well as an increase in wages for Argentine workers. In Argentina, the government controlled and paid the Catholic clergy. Their wages were also increased, and Peron authorized the building of new seminaries to train priests.

However, by Peron's second term, conditions in Argentina had changed. During the early 1950s, the nation found itself in the midst of an economic recession. Peron's wife, the charismatic Evita, was dying from cancer. In addition, the Roman Catholic pope, Pius XII, demanded that the government end its control of the clergy in Argentina and return authority to Rome. Peron was outraged and arrested many members of the Argentine clergy who supported the pope. Huge demonstrations broke out in Buenos Aires, churches were burned, and many demonstrators were killed by the Argentine armed forces. But Peron had lost most of his support, and in 1956 he was overthrown by the Argentine army.

A Vocation

Jorge did not stand on the sidelines during this upheaval. He attended Catholic action meetings, where priests spoke out against the Peron government. In addition, he joined demonstrators who called on the government to give up its control of the Argentine universities and hand them over to the Catholic Church. Jorge had been a supporter of Peron during the president's first term in office, but like so many other Argentines, he gradually turned against President Peron.

Meanwhile, Jorge had been excelling in his studies at the industrial school where he specialized in food chemistry. According to two of his classmates, "He was always many steps ahead of us." But Jorge did not keep all his learning to himself. "He supported us all the time if we had problems with any subjects; he always offered to assist."[6] At the same time, he was also strengthening his Catholic faith.

Then an incident occurred that changed his life forever. On September 21, 1953, he was going out to meet his girlfriend as well as some of his other friends. Along the way, Jorge passed a church and decided to go inside. In the quiet darkness that surrounded him, Jorge saw a priest and made up his mind to have the priest hear his confession. He later recalled:

> Something strange happened to me in that confession. I don't know what it was, but it changed my life. . . . I realized that they were waiting for me. That is the religious experience; the astonishment of meeting someone who has been waiting for you all along. From that moment on, for me, God is the One who. . . "springs it on you." . . . You want to find Him, but He finds you first.[7]

Shortly afterward, Jorge told some of his closest friends that he planned to finish the program to become a technical chemist, but he then planned to enter a Catholic seminary and study to become a priest. At first, when he told his parents, his mother was quite upset.

She had planned on his pursuing a professional career. Jorge then sought out his friend Father Pozzoli for his advice, and the priest agreed to talk to Jorge's parents. At last, his mother agreed, and Jorge entered the Buenos Aires diocesan seminary in March 1956.

Chapter 3

A YOUNG JESUIT

Jorge Bergoglio's first year in the seminary studying to be a Catholic priest almost proved to be his only year there. In summer 1957, he was struck by a life-threatening lung disease, called pleurisy, which endangered his breathing. Only after major surgery and the removal of part of his right lung, was Bergoglio able to survive. He also benefitted from the help of his old friend, Sister Dolores, who prayed with him and enabled him to endure the intense pain that his illness had caused. However, the loss of some lung tissue left Jorge permanently weakened, and he had to give up playing soccer. The surgery left Jorge only able to follow his favorite sport as an avid fan.

During his first year in the seminary, he faced another, quite different problem. At a wedding for a member of the Bergoglio family, he had met a beautiful young woman whose intelligence and charm had deeply attracted him. For a while, he considered leaving the seminary to pursue a relationship with her—something forbidden to Catholic priests. But, in the end, Jorge decided that his commitment to the priesthood was much more important, and he continued with his studies.

In the second year at the seminary, however, Bergoglio made another decision that changed the rest of his life. During his first year, he had met a number of Jesuits—members of the Society of Jesus—who ran the institution. So impressed was he with them and their way of life, that Bergoglio decided to become a Jesuit

In 1960, Bergoglio began studies at the Colegio Maximo, outside Buenos Aires. The Jesuit seminary's chapel is pictured above.

priest. This would involve him in a course of study that would take the next twelve years.

The Jesuit Life

The Society of Jesus had been founded in the 1500s by a Spanish nobleman named Ignatius of Loyola. Recovering from a severe wound that he had received on the battlefield, Ignatius began experiencing moments of religious inspiration. Eventually, he decided to give up his life, wealth, and warfare to devote himself to the spiritual life. Ignatius spent the next fifteen years as a homeless beggar, developing his relationship with God. Then he published a book called *The Spiritual Exercises*, providing advice to others who wanted to follow in his footsteps. This became the basis of the spiritual and intellectual training for men who joined the Jesuit Order.

Meanwhile, Ignatius had begun to attract many followers to his way of life. At its foundation were three vows that Jesuits were required to take—chastity, poverty, and obedience. Over the next three centuries, Jesuits became among the leading clergymen of Europe and the New World. Because of their learning and leadership qualities, some of them became advisers to Europe's monarchs. Others traveled to the Far East and the Americas, where they worked to convert native populations to Christianity.

Arriving in Argentina in the late sixteenth century, Jesuits established huge cattle ranches and became the founders of universities. They also worked closely with the chiefs of the local Guarani Indians establishing successful villages where Native Americans and Spanish settlers could live together in peace. Each town had its own craftsmen, orchards, church, and houses. The Jesuits themselves were not only spiritual leaders but practical men who could teach the Guarani ranching, farming, blacksmithing, and other skills.

In short, the Jesuits were men who lived very much in the world, while pursuing a spiritual and intellectual life, and dedicating themselves to helping the poor and

Ignatius of Loyola

Born in 1491, Ignatius's family were nobles who served the king and queen of Spain. He spent his early life as a soldier until he was wounded and returned home to Spain. After his spiritual life was transformed, he spent the next three years—from 1524 to 1527—studying and taking vows of poverty and chastity. Along with several other men, Ignatius went to Rome in 1537, where he was ordained a priest. Although he expected to go to the Middle East to begin converting Muslims to Christianity, Ignatius was asked by Pope Paul III to remain in Italy. There he founded the Jesuit Order and became its head in 1541, serving until his death in 1556. It was one of many groups of priests established inside the Catholic Church. These included the Franciscans, founded in 1223, and the Benedictines, founded in the sixth century. As the Jesuits grew, their members became teachers, missionaries, and political advisors.

disadvantaged. They encouraged the Guarani to preserve their age-old customs while, at the same time, teaching them about Christianity.

Along with twenty-five other young men, Jorge Bergoglio had decided to follow in the footsteps of the early Jesuit priests. He began attending the Colegio Maximo outside Buenos Aires in March 1960. In his first year, as a novice, he studied the Exercises. Then he was expected to carry out menial tasks—like cleaning and sweeping—in a local hospital. Novices also went on a pilgrimage for a month, living as homeless beggars. Finally, they taught children in nearby schools and improved their abilities in public speaking.[1]

While studying for the priesthood at the Colegio Maximo, Bergoglio lived in this room.

Over the next few years, Bergoglio received a broad education in courses such as literature, art, Latin, and Greek. He spent a year studying in Chile and another year in Spain. Along the way, Jorge's studies were interrupted by two years of teaching at the Colegio de la Inmaculada Concepcion in Santa Fe, Argentina. This was the first secondary school established by the Jesuits in Argentina, in 1610, and since then it had educated many of the most important leaders in the country. Bergoglio taught Spanish literature, psychology, and art to the students who attended the school.[2]

His teaching at the Colegio was considered so exemplary that for a short time Jorge became rector— (leader) of the secondary school—even before completing his studies as a Jesuit. After completing his studies in Spain—toward the end of his training in 1971—he was appointed master of novices (young men just entering the Jesuit Order).[3]

Changes in the Catholic Church

While Bergoglio was involved in his Jesuit training, the Catholic Church was going through a major transformation. In 1959, Pope John XXIII called the second Vatican Council. This was a meeting of Catholic cardinals from around the world in Rome that began in 1962 and continued until 1965. One of the goals of the pope and the council was to bring the Catholic religion more directly into the lives of Catholics. As a result, the council voted to change the centuries-old practice of priests celebrating the Mass in Latin—which

Pope John XXIII rides to the 21st Ecumenical Council of the Catholic Church. Vatican II addressed the church's role in the modern world.

most parishioners did not understand—and instead celebrating Mass in the native language of parishioners. Therefore, in Argentina, the Mass was celebrated in Spanish and in the United States in English. In addition, the Council put much greater emphasis on the important role of bishops and priests in their communities and not just inside the Church itself. The old hierarchy of bishops ruling their parishioners and their parish priests was to be replaced by more equality among all members of the Church.

The changes brought by Vatican II, as the Council was called, had a profound effect on Jorge Bergoglio, as well as other Jesuits. These were men who—like those Jesuits before them—had spent their lives working among the faithful, both rich and poor.[4]

In South America, a meeting of Catholic bishops at Medellin, Colombia, in 1968 sought to apply the decisions made at Vatican II to the parishes of Latin America. Most specifically, the Medellin Conference emphasized the commitment of the Church to the poor. The Catholic leaders believed that the Church must not only lead people away from sin but also from oppressive societies that kept poor people from improving their lives.

Many years later when he was cardinal of Buenos Aires, Jorge Bergoglio explained, "The option for the poor comes from the first centuries of Christianity. It's the Gospel itself. . . . It has always considered the poor

Bergoglio (left) attends Mass with the Jesuit Superior General Pedro Arrupe (right). He was ordained in 1969.

to be the treasure of the Church."[5] Shortly after the conference of bishops, Jorge Bergoglio was ordained a priest in the Catholic Church. It was December 1969, and he was almost thirty-three years old.

Chapter 4

CHAOS IN ARGENTINA

A s Father Jorge Bergoglio began his public ministry in the Society of Jesus, Argentina was poised on the brink of political chaos. The military *junta* (group) that ran the government had been unable to improve the economy. As a result, conditions among the poor in the cities and rural areas had grown even worse. There were no jobs available, housing conditions were growing worse, and the future looked even bleaker. The Catholic clergy was divided over how to respond to this situation. Some supported the government, believing that the military brought some stability to the nation. Others were far more radical, supporting guerillas that challenged the government by attacking military units and assassinating government ministers.

In the middle, there were men like Father Bergoglio. While he was committed to improving the lot of the poor, he believed that the more radical priests were simply

Once ordained into the priesthood, Father Bergoglio began his public ministry, aiding the poor in Argentina.

interested in bettering the people's material conditions. Bergoglio believed, on the other hand, that their spiritual life was also important, and that the Catholic Church should provide spiritual as well as political guidance. While believing that the poor should be liberated from their poverty, he also wanted to make sure the Catholic Church did not lose sight of the teachings of Christ. Therefore, he found himself in a middle ground between the conservatives and the radicals. The conservatives supported the government; the radicals believed in a liberation theology—focused mainly on liberating the poor from their miserable conditions.

Meanwhile, Father Bergoglio found himself in a unique position to influence the role of the Catholic Church and, more specifically, the Jesuits in the nation's future. Earlier in his career, he had worked as an assistant novice master in the Jesuit Order in Argentina; and in 1971, Bergoglio was named as the novice master. The number of young men becoming Jesuits had been declining, and part of his job was to increase the number of novices. In this effort, he succeeded, and soon afterward he was named an advisor to the Jesuit provincial—the head of the Argentine Order, becoming provincial himself in 1973. He was also teaching courses at the Colegio Maximo and assisting the Jesuit head of the college. All of this was a tribute to his gifts as a teacher, a leader, a spiritual advisor, and man respected by others for his sound judgment. It was very unusual for a young Jesuit only in his thirties.

Political Conditions in Argentina

Meanwhile, inside Argentina the military leaders had decided to permit elections for a new government. Since his ouster in the 1960s, Juan Peron had been living in exile in Spain. Nevertheless, millions of Argentines wanted him to return to run the country. Late in 1973, Peron overwhelmingly won the presidential election and began serving another term in the *Casa Rosada*— the Pink House, or presidential home. He was already seventy-eight years old and in poor health. Less than a year later, Peron was dead, and his wife Isabel took over the presidency.

Unfortunately, she proved to be a very weak leader. In various parts of Argentina, guerillas, some of them Communists, resumed their attacks on the government, which had briefly stopped after Peron's election. Isabella ordered out military death squads to stop the attacks. What followed was a period of political unrest, marked by assassinations, kidnappings, and murders.

While Argentines often looked to the Catholic Church to use its influence to help restore order, the Church itself was severely divided. Some priests backed the guerillas, while others stood firmly behind the government. Bergoglio tried to walk a middle path. While he believed that the Catholic Church should act as a champion of the poor, he also feared that "too much promotion of social justice could lead us to forget the religious dimension. . . ."[1] He called on Jesuits to forget their political squabbles, but many did not listen to him.

Led by priests such as Father Orlando Yorio and Father Franz Jalics, an important segment of the Jesuit Order called on the Church to support Liberation Theology and focus on the needs of the millions of impoverished Argentinians. Bergoglio was not insensitive to their plight, and he increased the number of missions serving people living in poverty. The number of novices had increased under Bergoglio's leadership, and they were ordered to serve in these missions as part of their training. But he always emphasized that this work must include an important spiritual dimension as well as an effort to free the poor from their grinding poverty. Otherwise, the Church could lose its way and become simply another political party calling for change—much like the Communists.

By 1976, however, a different kind of change was about to occur. Isabel Peron's government was overthrown by a military coup. Leaders of the army, navy, and air force took control of Argentina, imposing a harsh dictatorship that would be remembered for its brutal Dirty War.

The Dirty War

The Dirty War had actually begun under Isabel Peron's government in early 1976. She ordered her soldiers to use any means necessary to wipe out the Communist guerillas who were terrorizing part of the countryside. These guerillas were supported with money and military supplies by the Communist regime of Fidel Castro in Cuba. Peron's soldiers began a terrorist campaign of their own, rounding up guerillas, torturing them, and

Tanks and troops surrounded the government buildings in Buenos Aires after Argentine President Isabel Peron was overthrown.

executing them without trials. But it was not enough, and a military group, or junta, took over later that year, with Army General Jorge Videla becoming president of Argentina.

The junta remained in power for the next seven years. Following a National Reorganization Process, called *el Proceso*, they wanted to remake Argentine society. After the chaos of the Peron years, some Argentines initially

Dictatorships in South America

Argentina was among a number of countries in South America during the 1970s and 1980s where military dictatorships ruled. These included Uruguay, Brazil, Paraguay, and Chile.

In Chile, the elected president, Salvador Allende, had been overthrown and killed in 1973. Among those imprisoned were Michelle Bachelet and her mother. They were tortured, then released and exiled to East Germany.

Bachelet later returned to Chile in the 1980s. Chile's military dictator, Augusto Pinochet, eventually left office for a democratically elected government. Later, Bachelet served as minister of health, then defense minister, and was elected president in 2006. Bachelet was reelected in 2014.

were relieved, as the military shut down the law courts, limited free speech, outlawed political parties, and clamped a dictatorship onto the nation.

During that period, the junta also set up more than 300 facilities designed to imprison, torture, and execute people who were considered enemies of the state. These included not only guerillas, but teachers, journalists, pregnant women, priests, and students—anyone who seemed to disagree with the policies of the military regime. At least 9,000 people were killed in this so-called Dirty War. They were "disappeared," that is, removed from society never to be seen again. Among them were women who had been rounded up by the state—some of whom were pregnant. After they gave birth, their children were taken from them and given up for adoption. Soon afterward, most of the women were executed.

Others who opposed the government were simply assassinated. Among them was Bishop Enrique Angelleli, a strong supporter of Liberation Theology. Meanwhile Bergoglio's close friend Esther Balestrino de Careaga had become a leader of the Mothers of the Plaza de Mayo. This large group of women carried pictures of their adult children—many of them considered subversives by the regime—who had been disappeared. They demonstrated regularly at the Plaza de Mayo, calling on the junta to give them information about their children. Esther Balestrino de Careaga was eventually imprisoned by the regime, tortured, and like many others, she was dropped out of a military helicopter to her death.

The Church and the Dirty War

The Catholic Church, which had been divided before the military coup, continued to be divided during the Dirty War. Many Catholic leaders said later that they did not know about the full extent of the regime's brutal methods. Others who did know supported the military. According to *New Yorker* magazine reporter Jon Lee Anderson, "For the most part, the Church remained mute [silent] in public about what was going on. But some priests were directly involved in the repression, by all accounts, with military chaplains going so far as to bless the drugged bodies of suspected guerrillas marked for execution as they were loaded onto military planes, from which they were then hurled to their deaths, unconscious. . . ."[2]

What was Jorge Bergoglio's role in all of this? Observers disagree. One incident involving Bergoglio

Mothers of the children who "disappeared" during the Dirty War demonstrate at the Plaza de Mayo in 1982.

concerns Orlando Yorio and Franz Jalics, two priests who were serving the poor in a slum neighborhood of Buenos Aires. According to Bergoglio, he told the two priests that the military junta regarded their work as a threat to the government, and he ordered them to leave. When they disobeyed his order—violating their vows as Jesuits—he said that they had to resign from the Order. This apparently acted as a signal to the military regime that the two men were not going to be protected by the Church. Shortly afterward, they were rounded up and tortured, but later released.[3]

Yorio later said that Bergoglio had not done enough to help them. But Bergoglio explained that he "began to move immediately" to secure their release. Bergoglio met with Rafael Videla, head of the government, and Emilio Massera—a navy officer in the government—trying to secure their freedom. Later, after their release, Bergoglio said he helped them leave Argentina.[4]

These were not the only people he helped. Argentine Nobel Prize winner Adolfo Perez Esquivel—who was arrested by the junta—later said that Bergoglio "was not an accomplice of the dictatorship. . . .There were bishops who were accomplices of the Argentine dictatorship, but not Bergoglio." Another observer added that Bergoglio was constantly doing "as much as he could behind the scenes."[5]

This included hiding people targeted by the regime, arranging for them to get false passports and plane trips out of Argentina to other countries. "Bergoglio saved dozens of people, above all in the years 1976 to 1978, by sheltering them in the Maximo and filtering them abroad via a Jesuit-run international network of escape routes," according to author Austen Ivereigh.[6] He did all of this at great risk to his safety and perhaps even his life.

Chapter 5

IN THE CENTER OF CONFLICT

In 1979, Father Bergoglio completed his term as provincial in Argentina. Now he could focus his full attention on his role as rector of the Colegio Maximo. From this position he continued to have enormous influence on the Catholic Church and the Jesuit Order in Argentina.

According to Argentine author Elisabetta Piqué, Bergoglio did not stay aloof from his students, as other rectors had done. He was an "unconventional rector," who did everything that he asked the students to do. This included cooking, cleaning, and even taking care of the animals—pigs, cows, and chickens—that lived on the college campus.[1] Father Angel Rossi, who worked

Father Bergoglio (left) administers Mass with Father Carlos Cravena, Minister of the Colegio Maximo, sometime around 1976.

side by side with the rector, recalled that Bergoglio would help needy people who showed up at the Colegio Maximo by giving them food and other necessities. He would also send priests out to visit poor families to find out what they needed."[2]

Hero to the Poor

Bergoglio believed that Jesuits should not only be for the people but *of* the people. This involved caring for their spiritual and physical needs. It also meant that Jesuits were expected to work at the same tasks as the poor people of Argentina. As Pique explained, "Bergoglio becomes a kind of super-hero to the hundreds of working class children that surround the huge Colegio Maximo."[3]

One child remembered, "Padre Jorge was always concerned about what was happening in the area, so his home, the Colegio Maximo, was always our home. We studied Catechism there, and I learned what a cinema was." On Saturdays, the children would watch movies and leave with toys Bergoglio gave them because their parents could not afford to buy them. This child later went on to college and received a degree in business.[4]

While the military regime may have been successful in stopping the guerrillas, they had failed to improve the Argentine economy. As a result, many poor, working people were suffering. As Jesuit students visited families in the area, they discovered that many people could only afford a single daily meal. Bergoglio resolved to change this situation. He led the gathering of more than 100 pigs, cows, sheep, and beehives, and together with his Jesuit students he brought the food these animals produced to the tables of the poor.

In the early 1980s, Bergoglio enlisted a large group of volunteers to establish the *Casa del Nino* (house for children). According to author Austen Ivereigh, the Casa provided meals for 400 children each day. The students and faculty of the Colegio ate the same food that the children did, although, Ivereigh added, some of the professors complained.[5] But they learned that Bergoglio could be a tough taskmaster when it came to carrying out what he believed were the Christian principles proclaimed by Jesus Christ two thousand years earlier. Everyone was equal, whether they were rich or poor, weak or powerful, young or old.

Bergoglio later recalled that he did not always listen carefully to those who disagreed with him—especially when he was engaged in carrying out his mission. In addition to the Casa, Bergoglio solicited donations to build a night school for adults, a technical school, as well as providing college scholarships for children. As Father Miguel Yanez recalled, "We really made a difference. Today those kids are teachers and doctors, or they've got degrees and have really got on in society."[6]

But he never forgot their spiritual lives. Every Sunday, young Jesuits would spread out into the *barrios* (slums) of Buenos Aires searching for children and taking them to Mass. Recalling Bergoglio years later, one of these children said, "When he was at Sunday Mass, he would ask us to pray for him. The times he wasn't there to say

Thanks to a poor national economy, many Argentines were impoverished. Bergoglio worked tirelessly to help them.

Mass, we missed him."[7] His position as rector did not confine Bergoglio to the college. Under his leadership, five new churches were built in the area. Their grounds became the center of organized soccer championships for the children. But he also used the occasion to enrich their spiritual lives, because at soccer games priests would hand out holy pictures to the players.

"What did he have that was different from the other Jesuits?" asked Nora Castro who knew him during this period. "First of all, humility, kindness, the desire to help in different and splendid ways—and I'm not the only one who says so. He didn't like pretending or showing off. He was simple in soul and in deed."[8]

Political Crisis

Father Bergoglio's commitment to his principles was about to be tested by a series of crises that engulfed Argentina and the Jesuits. In spring 1982, the military junta decided to begin a military operation in the Falklands (known by the Argentinians as the Malvinas) off Argentina's west coast. These islands had been claimed by Argentina for many years, although they had primarily British settlers and they were administered by the British government.

According to military historian, Kennedy Hickman, the "operation was designed to draw attention away from human rights and economic issues at home by bolstering national pride and giving teeth to the nation's long-held claim to the islands."[9] On April 2, Argentine soldiers landed on the Falklands, and two days later they had taken control of the capital, Port Stanley. It was a speedy victory, but unfortunately for Argentina it was just the beginning of the war.

British Prime Minister Margaret Thatcher ordered a naval task force to the south Atlantic to recapture the islands. After several naval battles that cost both sides some ships, the British landed on May 21. Although the British ships covering the landings were bombed and strafed by Argentine aircraft, the invasion continued. British troops defeated the Argentinian army and took control of the towns of Darwin and Goose Green. As more British soldiers landed, their commander, Major General Jeremy Moore, ordered an attack on Port Stanley. On June 14, the Argentine military, under General Mario Menendez, surrendered and the war was over.

Bergoglio had opposed the Falklands War, and after the defeat of Argentina's army, most people stopped supporting the military government. The leaders themselves realized that they must resign and hand over power to a civilian government. In October 1983, democratic elections were finally held, and Raul Alfonsin was elected president of Argentina.

Religious Crisis

The political crisis in Argentina was followed by a religious crisis among the Jesuits. After Bergoglio's term as provincial ended, most people expected that he would do what others in the same position had done before him—retire from the center of the Jesuit Order in Argentina. But as rector of the Colegio Maximo,

Bergoglio had been busier than ever. However, his ideas for the proper role that Jesuit priests should play among the poor were not supported by everyone in the Order. In addition, some Jesuit leaders believed that Bergoglio should have been openly critical of the military government and its brutal policies of

Falklands Naval Air War

A large part of the Falklands War was fought on the sea and in the air, as Britain tried to isolate the Argentine army on the islands, and Argentina tried to keep open its army's supply lines. Argentine planes followed the British naval taskforce as it approached the Falklands and another nearby island, South Georgia. British forces sunk the Argentine submarine ARA *Santa Fe* in April, prior to recapturing South Georgia at the end of April. The British submarine HMS Conqueror fired a series of torpedoes that scored direct hits on the cruiser ARA *General Belgrano* and sunk the ship. As a result, the Argentine surface fleet did not reappear during the war. But the Argentine Air Force continued its attacks on the British fleet. The HMS *Sheffield*, HMS *Ardent*, HMS *Antelope*, and HMS *Coventry* were all sunk. Nevertheless, the Argentine soldiers on the Falklands had been cut off, and in the face of superior British forces, they surrendered.

Argentine losses were 649 killed, 1,068 wounded, and 11,313 captured. British losses were 258 killed and 777 wounded.

kidnapping and murder. They wanted to become more involved in politics.

Finally, Bergoglio's success at bringing many young men into the Jesuit Order convinced some older Jesuits that he would transform the Church's entire mission in Argentina. These young Jesuits supported Bergoglio and his leadership, believing that they should be "for" and "of" the people not simply guiding them from above.

Father Peter-Hans Kolvenbach, the newly elected leader of the worldwide Jesuit Order, believed that the time had come to intervene in this situation. He decided that the new provincial should be Father Victor Zorzin, a man who disagreed with Bergoglio's policies. In 1986, Zorzin ordered Bergoglio to take a leave of absence from the Colegio Maximo. He was ordered to Germany to study for a doctoral degree. In his absence, Zorzin also began to remove the Jesuits loyal to Bergoglio from the churches he had established.

Meanwhile, while Bergoglio was in Germany he had a religious experience that brought him back to Argentina. Inside a Jesuit church in the German city of Augsburg, he saw a painting of Mary, the mother of Jesus. In the painting, Mary receives a thread of knots from one angel, then she unties the knots, and hands the thread to another angel. For Bergoglio, this seemed to be a sign or symbol of what he must do. He had gone to Germany because a Jesuit was expected to obey the orders of this provincial. Now, it seemed that God was ordering him back to Argentina to untie the knots of the Jesuit Order there.

Return and Exile

After his return, Bergoglio was ordered by Father Zorzin to teach at another college and continue his doctoral work. By 1987, Argentina was in the midst of great turmoil. The

British troops surrender to Argentines in this photo from the Falklands War. However, Argentina was ultimately defeated.

Alfonsin government had done nothing to improve the economy. High inflation—which meant that Argentina's currency could buy less because prices had risen so high—was hurting many people. Trials were underway for leaders who had carried on the Dirty War, creating conflict within Argentina's society. Indeed, young officers had carried out rebellions to protest the trials while on the other side guerilla bands had attacked military instillations.

Throughout 1987, Father Zorzin continued his effort to isolate Bergoglio. But the provincial met serious resistance from younger Jesuits who supported Bergoglio. As an indication of the popular support that Bergoglio enjoyed, he was elected to represent the Argentine province at an important meeting in Rome. His job was to join other representatives, reporting on the conditions of the Jesuit Order in their regions. Zorzin and his supporters were upset that Bergoglio had been chosen. Over the next two years, they continued to oppose his policies, creating conflict within the Jesuit Order in Argentina. Finally, in April 1990, Zorzin—with the support of the Jesuit leaders in Rome—ordered that Bergoglio and his supporters should leave Buenos Aires. Some were sent to Europe, while Bergoglio himself was sent to a Jesuit center in Cordoba, Argentina—many miles from the capital.[10]

There he was ordered not to contact any of the men he had worked with in the past. It appeared that his leadership among the Jesuits had come to an end.

Chapter 6

ARCHBISHOP OF BUENOS AIRES

S oon after he was elected pope, Pope Francis delivered the *Evangelii Guadium* (The Joy of the Gospel) in November 2013:

The great danger in today's world, pervaded as it is by consumerism, is the desolation and anguish born of a complacent yet covetous heart, the feverish pursuit of frivolous pleasures, and a blunted conscience. Whenever our interior life becomes caught up in its own interests and concerns, there is no longer room for others, no place for the poor. God's voice is no longer heard, the quiet joy of his love is no longer felt, and the desire to do good fades. . . . Jesus wants us to touch human misery, to touch the suffering flesh of others. Whenever we do so, our lives become wonderfully complicated and

Cardinal Antonio Quarracino, who was named cardinal of Buenos Aires by Pope John Paul II, was a powerful ally to Father Bergoglio.

we experience intensely what it is to be a people, to
be part of a people.[1]

This statement summed up an approach to the
people of Buenos Aires that Father Bergoglio had
followed throughout his entire career. It had been
honed in the barrios around his church and deepened
during his exile in Cordoba. There a change had also
come over him. In the past, while he cared deeply for
the priests who worked with him, he did not always
listen carefully to what they said. He made up his mind
and acted. But in Cordoba, he had learned to listen,
especially as he heard the confessions of the priests at
the Jesuit center there. And he used this newly found
skill upon his return to Buenos Aires.

A Powerful Ally

Bergoglio's road back was as much due to luck as
to anything else. In 1990, Pope John Paul II named
Antonio Quarracino, the archbishop of La Plata, as the
new cardinal of Buenos Aires. Cardinal Quarracino was
a close friend of the pope who also liked the fact that
the cardinal was an advocate of the working classes and
a strong supporter of social programs for the poor. In
addition, Quarracino was a friend and ally of Argentina's
new president, Carlos Menem, a member of the Peronist
Party. Menem served as president from 1989 to 1999.

Quarracino knew Bergoglio and admired the work he
had done with the poor while serving as Jesuit provincial
and as rector at the Colegio Maximo. In 1990, the new

cardinal asked Bergoglio to provide religious instruction to a number of priests in Quarracino's old parish, La Plata. Father Bergoglio selected a story from the New Testament about the Good Samaritan. This was a man who stopped to help a wounded traveler along the roadside, when so many other people who had seen him simply passed by and did nothing. Bergoglio's message was that everyone will be judged by how much they do for the poor and the helpless. And, he added, we must help them one person at a time, with compassion and care.

Bergoglio's work in La Plata further convinced Quarracino that he needed the Jesuit in Buenos Aires. However, it was not an easy thing to accomplish. There was still strong opposition to him among the Jesuit leaders in Buenos Aires, and this influenced the bishops in Rome who had to approve his appointment. Quarracino, however, worked around this opposition, although it took a year and a half, and finally secured Pope John Paul's approval to appoint Bergoglio.

Auxiliary Bishop of Buenos Aires

In 1992, at age 55, Bergoglio became one of five auxiliary bishops (assistants) to Cardinal Quarracino. Immediately, the cardinal put him in charge of Flores. It was the poorest area of Buenos Aires, with forty-five parishes to manage. Father Carlos Accaputo, the priest who later became a close associate of Bergoglio, recalled that he was at first skeptical of the new auxiliary bishop. He had heard the rumors that Bergoglio had not given enough support to Yorio and Jalics in their efforts to help the poor, and that he had refused to stand up to the military regime. "On the day of his. . .ordination [as auxiliary bishop] I go to Mass," recalled Father Accaputo, "and begin to see that people go to greet him and I discover that there are very poor people there, people from the district of San Miguel where he had worked [before]. I realized that something didn't fit, what was happening?" Later Bergoglio came to talk with Accaputo and asked the priest to work for him.[2]

Bergoglio demonstrated almost immediately that he was different from other Church leaders. While they

Cardinal Quarracino

Antonio Quarracino was born in Italy in 1923, but his parents brought him to Argentina at age four. After becoming a priest in 1945, he taught theology at the Universidad Catolica (Catholic University) in Argentina. Pope John XXIII appointed him a bishop in 1962, and he served in Buenos Aires, and later in the Archdiocese of La Plata.

In the early 1990s, he became cardinal, archbishop of Buenos Aires and head of the Catholic Church in Argentina. Cardinal Quarracino was strongly opposed to homosexuality, saying that lesbians and gay men should be segregated and kept apart from other people. Nevertheless, he was a very outgoing and friendly man, who often appeared on television and initiated close ties with Jews in Argentina. He also set up a painting in the Cathedral of Buenos Aires to memorialize the Holocaust—the massacre of six million Jews by the Nazis during World War II. Cardinal Quarracino died of heart disease in 1998.

were assigned a chauffeur driven car, Bergoglio preferred to walk, ride the subway, or take the bus. He spent much of his time with parish priests, like Guillermo Marco, learning about the problems he faced. "He'd come to our parish a lot," Marco recalled, "and he would ask me to walk home with him so, he said, he could get to know his diocese and what a young priest like me was thinking."[3]

He worked this way with other priests, as well. After getting up at 4 a.m. every morning and devoting time to prayer, he would eat breakfast and then sit by his phone personally answering any calls from parish priests. "They would get straight through to him. Every priest in the diocese was given his number," Marco explained. "He didn't delegate much to his [assistants]," Marco added, "so everyone went straight to Bergoglio. He's a man with a strong sense of power."[4] Bergoglio, however, had learned to ask for advice from other people on his management team who met with him every two weeks. But when it came to the final decisions, there was no vote among the team, Marco added, he would make the decisions himself.[5]

Father Augusto Zampini, a parish priest, added, "The way [Bergoglio] implemented change was consultation, long process, participation—parishes, priests. . . . He made it clear he did not want to impose; he wanted things to emerge." In addition, added another associate, Federico Wals, Bergoglio involved the congregation

One of Pope Francis's most admired qualities is that he has never put on airs. Even as an auxiliary bishop, he continued to ride the subway.

because "[he] felt that if you didn't do it that way, you would end up with a Church that's too focused on itself."[6]

Bergoglio did not stop with Catholic congregations. He went to mosques where Muslims in Buenos Aires prayed. He had conversations with Jewish rabbis, like Abraham Skorka, who later recalled, "He can dialogue with anyone who speaks with honesty and respect even if he does not agree with them. He'll listen to a woman tussling with abortion [strongly opposed by the Catholic Church] and suffer with her. He has empathy. He has a very important listening capability. That doesn't mean he will change his mind."[7] Bergoglio even stopped to talk with prostitutes on the streets and hear their confessions. "No doubt I will one day appear in the newspapers," he laughed.[8]

Bergoglio's goal was always to bring Christianity to the people. As a result, he also held large outdoor Masses, attended by many thousands of people. As Wals put it, "He wanted to make the Church visible outside its buildings, which is why Buenos Aires developed some very interesting outdoor events. The most important Masses here don't take place inside the cathedral, but in the square." In 2001, Bergoglio celebrated an important Easter ritual, washing the feet of common people, just as Christ had done two thousand years earlier. He went to a hospital in Buenos Aires and with water from a jar washed the feet of twelve acquired immunodeficiency syndrome (AIDS) patients.[9]

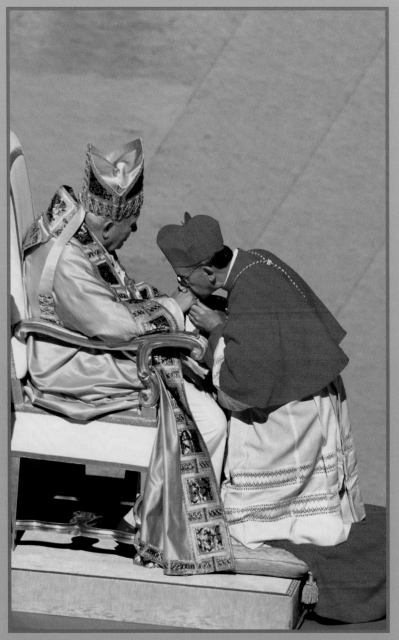

Pope John Paul II nominated Bergoglio as Cardinal Quarracino's successor at the Papal Consistory in 1998.

One of the outdoor parades commemorated the Virgin Mary, with people carrying her image. A priest recalled that he had left Bergoglio earlier and didn't expect him at the parade. But one of the marchers spotted a man wearing a poncho. "Isn't that the bishop?" she said to the priest. "And indeed so he was, with a rosary in his hand. I was surprised, because as Bishop he could have made it evident that he was accompanying us but he hadn't said anything and had mingled with the people."[10]

Archbishop of Buenos Aires

Bergoglio's commitment to the people was being put to a stern test under the government of Carlos Menem. The economy was still struggling, although Argentines at the top of the income scale seemed to be growing even richer. In 1996, a group of priests from the slums staged a hunger strike to protest the building of an exit ramp from a new highway that would cause the demolition of several streets of houses. The strike continued during the hot summer months, fully covered by the television media, and strongly backed by Bergoglio. He continually visited the priests and convinced Quarracino to show his support for them. Eventually, Bergoglio convinced the government to put the exit ramp somewhere else in return for the priests' agreement that they would end the strike.

The Menem government was, however, furious with Bergoglio for the position he had taken on the highway project. Menem expected the Church to support the government's policies. Unlike in other South American countries, Catholic priests were paid employees of the government. But this did not sway Bergoglio. When two government bureaucrats came to his office, offering a large sum of money to fund projects that might help the poor, Bergoglio refused. The bureaucrats had implied that the Church would only receive half the money while the rest must be given to them as bribes.

Bergoglio refused to be bought by Menem's government, which was soon afterward exposed as being filled with corruption. But he did not win himself any friends for taking such an independent stand. As a result, when Cardinal Quarracino decided that he wanted Bergoglio chosen as his successor, government leaders tried to lobby Rome to prevent the appointment. But, once again, the cardinal succeeded in outwitting the government as well as powerful clergymen in Rome and persuaded Pope John Paul II to approve Bergoglio's appointment in 1997. The cardinal, who was suffering at the time from severe heart disease, died less than a year later. In 1998, Jorge Bergoglio became the new archbishop of Buenos Aires.

Chapter 7

CHURCH AND STATE IN CRISIS

S oon after becoming archbishop, Bergoglio faced a crisis that rocked the Church in Argentina. His predecessor, Cardinal Quarracino, had been a close friend of the Trusso family, one of Argentina's most prominent and wealthiest families. Father Alfredo Trusso, for example, was a religious leader. Another member of the family, Francisco Trusso, was the Argentine ambassador to the Vatican, and three of his sons were directors of a large bank, Banco de Credito Provincial (BCP).

Unknown to most Argentines, BCP had helped Archbishop Cardinal Quarracino financially by arranging to pay some of his credit card bills as well as first class airplane tickets and expensive hotel rooms when he traveled. The bank also loaned the Church money for some of its projects. In return, Quarracino had used his influence to arrange for a large military pension fund to deposit some of its money with the BCP. What most people did not know, however, was that the bank was in a dire financial condition.

According to Father Guillermo Marco, a close associate of Cardinal Quarracino, "At one point there was a run on the . . . bank. So one of the sons went to the [military pension fund] and said the Archbishop wanted to borrow $10 million. . . . When the lenders went to see Quarracino to get him to confirm this, and get the necessary paperwork signed, the Archbishop's secretary, Monsigneur Roberto Marcial Toledo, told them Quarracino was busy." Toledo said he would ask the Archbishop to sign the paperwork and took the documents. He later returned with the paperwork bearing Quarracino's signature, which, as it turns out, he had forged.[1] Later, the bank went bankrupt and the pension fund went to the Church and asked for the money back. But the money was not there. Apparently, the bank had tried to use the money to avoid bankruptcy. Several members of the Trusso family later went to prison.

Cardinal Quarracino was extremely embarrassed, and stress from the scandal may have led to his death shortly afterward. The case of the Church's involvement in the Trusso bank failure then went into the courts. The presiding judge in the case ordered the police to raid the diocesan headquarters and remove financial records. Bergoglio dealt with the problem immediately, calling in a team of leading accountants to carefully go through the financial records and make all necessary recommendations to improve the Church's financial procedures. In addition, he tightened up the rules governing how the Church could spend money and where the Church could make financial investments. "Bergoglio's thoroughness in the paperwork he handed over to the court meant his reputation was enhanced by the way he handled the whole affair," Marco added.[2]

Unfortunately, this was not enough to put an end to the financial crisis looming over Argentina. Other institutions found themselves in the same position as the Trusso bank—trying desperately to stay afloat. The Menem government was also struggling, having borrowed too much money from international banks and unable to pay back the loans.

Serving the Underserved

In 2000, President Menem finished his second term as Argentina's leader, and he was replaced after a general election by President Fernando de la Rúa. The new president promised to improve the economy, but there was little he could do. Government social services for the poor began to shrink, government employees were laid off, and middle class incomes were declining. Like a row of dominoes falling, this led to less consumer spending, businesses closing, and eventually massive unemployment. As banks teetered on the edge of

In 2001, social disturbances hit many areas of Argentina, as the government introduced unpopular economic austerity measures.

bankruptcy, the de la Rúa government froze bank accounts and ordered that depositors could withdraw no more than $250 from their accounts.

As Argentina faltered, the Catholic Church led by Archbishop Bergoglio stepped in to strengthen the social safety net in a massive effort to open soup kitchens for the poor, build health clinics, and establish drug rehab programs. As government financing of schools declined, the Church began a program to open twenty-two new schools over the next ten years.

Bergoglio usually preferred to work behind the scenes. But Father Marco helped convince him that the time had come to open a press office. Word of his efforts began to appear in the newspapers with pictures of Archbishop Bergoglio as he roamed among the people of his diocese. The press also covered his warnings to Menem and de la Rúa that more must be done to fulfill the needs of the lower middle class and the poor. This was a constant theme of Bergoglio's.

As he once said:

> "... it is our duty to share our food, clothing, health, and education with our brothers. Some may say, 'This priest is a communist!' That's not it. What I am saying is pure Gospel [the words of Jesus Christ], and be careful, because we are going to be judged by this. When Jesus comes to judge us ... He will say to some, ... 'Every time you helped the poor you helped me.' But He will say to others, 'Go away, because I was hungry and you gave me nothing to eat.' And He will also condemn us for the sin of blaming the government

for poverty, when it is a responsibility we must all assume to the extent we can."[3]

Nevertheless, Argentines did blame the government. Unemployment inside the country was approaching fifty percent of working people. Men and women, who had once been employed, were reduced to trying to sell pieces of cardboard that they had taken from garbage pails. Eighteen million people were suddenly reduced to poverty, while another nine million lived on under $1 per day.

Large crowds gathered in the streets of Buenos Aires and other cities demanding that President de la Rúa do something. They brought out cooking pans and banged them as a show of dissatisfaction with the government. The president's only response was to call out the military to disperse the crowds, leading to some protestors being killed and others wounded.

Unable to stop the protests, the president resigned and fled the capital. Over the next two weeks, three more presidents would be appointed only to quickly resign. Finally, the government declared bankruptcy, stating that it was unable to repay its debts. This cut off all financial help from abroad and plunged the nation even further into crisis.

The New Cardinal

While the crisis was underway, Archbishop Bergoglio flew to Rome. There in 2001 Pope John Paul II appointed him cardinal of Buenos Aires. He was one of forty-four new cardinals named by the pope. At this time, the long

John Paul II served as pope for more than twenty-five years. In 2014, Pope Francis declared the conservative pope a saint.

Pope John Paul II

Karol Jozef Wojtyla, the future pope, was born in Wadowice, Poland, in 1920. When Karol was only nine, his mother died, and three years later he lost his brother. After entering Jagiellonian University in 1938, Wojtyla was forced to leave a year later. Following the Nazi invasion of Poland and their quick conquest of the country in 1939, they closed the university. During World War II, Wojtyla secretly attended a Catholic seminary in Krakow, Poland, where he studied to become a priest.

After his ordination as a priest in 1946, he studied in Rome and in 1958—at the early age of thirty-eight—he became auxiliary bishop of Krakow. Later, he was appointed archbishop of the city and became a cardinal in 1967. His career was similar to Father Jorge Bergoglio's several decades later in Argentina. Widely respected by other cardinals because of his stand against Communism in Poland, his wide learning, and influential sermons, Cardinal Wojtyla was elected pope in 1978.

At age fifty-eight, he was among the youngest popes and the first from Poland. Serving as pope until his death in 2005, John Paul II traveled widely. A man of great charm and charisma, he attracted a huge following among Christians across the world. But he was also known for his conservatism—his opposition to abortion, contraception, homosexual relationships, and Liberation Theology. John Paul II also tried to centralize the running of the Church as much as possible in the Vatican—reducing the power of local bishops.

papacy of John Paul II was nearing its end. The pope was very ill with Parkinson's Disease—a serious brain disorder that includes trembling, eventual paralysis, and death. Meanwhile, the Catholic Church was in the midst of a severe crisis as evidence appeared regarding a number of priests who had molested little boys, many of them parishioners in their churches. Among them was Father Marcial Maciel, a Mexican priest, who was accused of being a drug addict and child molester.

While this crisis was rocking the foundations of the Church, Bergoglio flew back home where he began to work with the new President Eduardo Duhalde and social groups across Argentina to stem the economic depression. Throughout the nation, those who were still able to help the poor and unemployed worked together with the new president and the new cardinal. An estimated 2,000 volunteer organizations launched an enormous relief effort providing food, health care, transportation, and emotional support to millions who were struggling. Bergoglio sent volunteers into the streets to bring in anyone to the churches who was in need of care. Catholic parishioners were also urged to bring in what food and clothing they could to Masses held throughout the country.

It was a situation similar to the Great Depression that had gripped the United States and other parts of the world in the 1930s. Millions were thrown out of work, and there were no government programs to help them. As a result, volunteer organizations, private charities,

As cardinal, Bergoglio worked with President Eduardo Duhalde to address the needs of Argentina's poor.

and the churches stepped in to rescue individuals and their families from starvation. The same thing occurred in Argentina, as the lines waiting for food at Church soup kitchens grew longer and longer.

As a result of the crisis, *Dialogo Argentino* (Argentine Dialogue) began. Bergoglio believed that there were three elements that lead to cooperation in society: transcendence, or a closeness with God, diversity among its population, and a focus on the future.

For years, Bergoglio had criticized Argentine society for being polarized—rich against poor, one political party against another. Now he saw different groups coming together to rescue society. This massive effort helped save Argentina.

Chapter 8

A CARDINAL OF THE PEOPLE

arly in 2005, a terrible fire ripped through a nightclub in Buenos Aires. The fire at the Republica de Cromanon club killed as many as 200 people, injuring 1,500 others. Among the earliest to rush to the burning club was Cardinal Bergoglio. Along with his priests, he brought comfort to the relatives of those who had died and walked among the injured providing words of support. Meanwhile emergency care workers helped them into ambulances that sped to nearby hospitals. Investigations into the causes of the disaster revealed that the owners had allowed too many people inside, while locking safety exits to exclude those who tried to come in without paying. This prevented those inside the club from fleeing to safety. The club owners had also paid off local officials to allow them to ignore safety measures that might have saved lives.

Later in 2005, Bergoglio spoke to hundreds of local residents who crowded into a cathedral to remember the dead. "Distracted city," he said, "spread-out city, selfish city: cry! You need to be purified by tears. . . . And let us ask the Lord to touch each of our hearts. . . ."[1]

Bergoglio memorialized those affected by a tragic fire, in a 2005 Mass at which he implored listeners to be purified by tears.

A New Pope

Soon after the terrible nightclub fire, the Catholic Church mourned the loss of Pope John Paul II, who died after serving almost twenty-seven years as pope in 2005. He was one of the longest-serving popes in history. Along with other cardinals across the world, Bergoglio headed to Rome. On April 8, he attended a funeral for Pope John Paul II, which was followed soon afterward by a conclave of the cardinals to elect his successor. Many of the participants supported Cardinal Joseph Ratzinger. A German, he had worked closely with John Paul II in Rome for many years. Cardinal Ratzinger was a published author, was considered a leading Catholic theologian, and he had served as a member of the Curia—the Church's governing body.

In addition to Ratzinger, some of the cardinals were reportedly favoring Cardinal Carlo Martini, as well as several Latin American cardinals, including Bergoglio. But at this time, rumors began to circulate again that Bergoglio had somehow been involved in the arrests of Yorio and Jalics. What's more, after Jalics wanted to come back to Argentina—after leaving the country in the 1980s—it was rumored Bergoglio had played a role in preventing Jalics from returning.

According to Bergoglio's biographer, Austen Ivereigh, one American cardinal later told him, "we all knew the allegations, and we knew they weren't true."[2]

As the cardinals began the process of voting for a new pope, the first ballot gave no candidate the votes he needed to win. By the end of the voting the following day, Ratzinger had reached 72 votes (with 77 needed for victory) while Bergoglio had 40. At this point, Bergoglio decided to support Ratzinger. According to Ivereigh, he liked Cardinal Ratzinger and believed he should be pope. What's more, Bergoglio felt that he was not experienced enough to become pope himself. It was also not time, at least not yet, for a Latin American pope.[3]

In April 2005, Cardinal Ratzinger became the first German pope since the eleventh century, Pope Benedict XVI.

Bergoglio's List

Gonzalo Mosca had fled the dictatorship in Uruguay, only to find himself hunted by the military junta once he crossed the border into Argentina. "I thought they would kill me at any moment," he said following a government attack on the place he was staying. Father Bergoglio heard about Mosca's plight and stepped in to give him sanctuary at the Colegio Maximo.

There were soldiers on patrol near the Colegio, but Bergoglio had decided to risk arrest to save Mosca. "He gave me instructions: 'If they stop us, tell them you're going to a spiritual retreat. Try to keep yourself a bit hidden.'" Mosca added: "He made me wonder if he really understood the trouble he was getting into. If they grabbed us together, they would have marched us both off." Later, Bergoglio helped Mosca reach the airport and an airplane took him to Brazil. He was only one of many saved by Bergoglio. A movie is currently being made called "Bergoglio's List," about the list of people he saved during the Dirty War.[4]

Argentine Politics

In 2003, Nestor Kirchner had been elected president of Argentina. He had formerly served as the mayor of Rio Gallegos and later governor of Santa Cruz province. During Kirchner's presidency, the Argentine economy improved. Nevertheless, the conflicts within Argentine society—an issue that Bergoglio had always spoken out against—grew deeper. Kirchner accused Bergoglio of quietly supporting the military dictatorship, calling Cardinal Bergoglio "the true representative of the opposition."[5]

Bergoglio believed that Kirchner was simply trying to create dissension among different groups in Argentina. It was a technique that had been used by Juan Peron—whom Kirchner had strongly supported. He would select enemies whom he said were threatening the country and galvanize his political supporters to rally against them. Kirchner did the same thing, accusing certain Supreme Court justices of corruption and forcing them to resign. He also forced out high-ranking military officers associated with the Dirty War. All of these things angered Bergoglio, who wanted to bring the nation together after the economic collapse and the military dictatorship. In addition, he believed that Kirchner should spend more of his time helping the poor and dealing with the types of corruption that had led to the nightclub fire.

Liberation Theology

One reason that Cardinal Bergoglio was such a strong opponent of President Kirchner was his strong support

Bergoglio was at odds with President Nestor Kirchner, who fed his power by creating dissension among different factions in Argentina.

for Liberation Theology. This movement believed that there were many passages in the Bible that called for a just society that benefited the poor. Liberation Theology had gained many followers in Latin America, where a small number of wealthy dominated society, and millions lived in poverty.

This movement pointed to the Bible to justify serving the poor. In the book of Luke, from the New Testament, Mary, the mother of Jesus, states: "He has brought down rulers from their thrones/but has lifted up the humble/ He has filled the hungry with good things/but has sent the rich away empty."

Bergoglio's attitude toward Liberation Theology had evolved since he served as head of the Jesuits in Argentina and rector of the Colegio Maximo. As his biographer Paul Vallely has explained, the change was due in part to worldwide political conditions. In the 1970s, Communism led by the Soviet Union was a powerful international force. It was a godless system that called for the overthrow of elected governments to create a society to benefit workers. Bergoglio feared Communism, and he believed that Liberation Theology was too closely allied with it. This was the reason that he had not supported Yorio and Jalics when they wanted to establish a center in the slums. He feared that they were going around the Church and Christianity to help the poor, allying themselves too closely with the Communists.[6]

But by the 1990s, the Soviet Union had disappeared, and world Communism was in retreat. In the meantime,

Bergoglio became an advocate for the mentally ill. In this photo, he is shown talking with residents of the Borda psychiatric hospital.

Bergoglio had been serving as a bishop and later archbishop of Buenos Aires. "Over his eighteen years as bishop and archbishop in Buenos Aires," Vallely wrote, " . . . one priest estimated, Bergoglio must have personally talked to at least half the people in the slum in visits where he would just turn up, wander the alleyways, and chat to the locals. . . ." In addition, Bergoglio realized that priests were not there to help—as people who were smarter and better off might donate their time and money to the poor. "He doesn't see the poor as people he can help but rather as people from whom he can learn," explained Father Marco.[7]

As Vallely added that Bergoglio had begun to see what the Liberation Theology movement had recognized much earlier, "what the poor need is not charity but justice."[8] He had always been willing to provide them with charity. But that was not enough. Bergoglio now realized that the political system must represent the poor to a much greater degree for justice to be theirs and their lives to improve. Capitalism, he believed, enriched only the wealthy. In its place an elected government must provide greater opportunities for the poor to find justice through education, jobs, and higher wages.

In support of his beliefs, Cardinal Bergoglio helped the very poor in Buenos Aires who combed through trash barrels at night to find something they might sell for even a few pennies. As Frederico Wals, who served as the cardinal's public relations director explained, "Bergoglio helped them to form a union and to turn this work into something from which they can make a decent living. He wanted to help them protect their rights."[9]

And he went a step further. Bergoglio believed that local beliefs and customs should have an important place side by side with more traditional Catholic religious teachings. One of these local beliefs centered around Our Lady of Caacupé, a local saint revered by many people. Bergoglio supported a popular movement in Buenos Aires to carry a statue of the saint down the streets of the barrios. He also celebrated a special Mass to honor the saint. "Look how far the children from the villa (barrio) have come!" he said when hundreds of them joined their parents in the Catholic cathedral.[10]

Cardinal Bergoglio had proven himself a religious leader quite different from others inside the Catholic Church.

Chapter 9

FIGHTING CRIME AND CORRUPTION

I n the barrios of Buenos Aires and across the rest of Argentina, the number of poor was growing. The people who could only afford to live in slum housing had increased by over seventy percent between 2004 and 2010. Many of the poor were also being exploited by gangsters involved in drug dealing, prostitution, and gambling. When the barrio priests, led by Father Pepe Di Paola, spoke out against the drug dealers in 2009, they threatened to kill him. Padre Pepe, as he was called, had spent a decade increasing services for the poor. Pepe and the other slum priests had established a high school, trade school, soup kitchens, drug prevention programs, rehabilitation programs, and many new chapels to serve the barrio residents in Buenos Aires.

One night, Padre Pepe was stopped by a stranger in the street, who threatened him with death. In response, more than 350 priests announced their support for Padre Pepe. He called a news conference to publicize and explain how the gangsters were threatening his work in the barrios. Padre Pepe and Cardinal Bergoglio strolled together through the streets of the barrios to show the world that the slum priest had full Church support. The situation received international attention, and Bergoglio followed it up by increasing the commitment of the Church to assist the poor.[1]

Fighting Gambling and Exploitation

Meanwhile, Cardinal Bergoglio had begun to focus attention on the growth of gambling establishments in the city. These included bingo, slot machines, and lotteries, which attracted the poor who spent money they could ill afford, hoping to win a large payoff. Political leaders had often permitted gambling to increase in return for bribes by the wealthy casino owners. This situation changed due to political pressure by the cardinal and other Church leaders, and their support for newspaper publicity about political corruption as well as mass demonstrations in Buenos Aires. As a result, the city government in Buenos Aires eventually stepped in and began regulating the gambling industry.

Bergoglio had become a master at using television and newspaper publicity as well as mass organizing and political pressure to help the poor in Argentina.

Another issue that drew his attention was the exploitation of women. Some had been brought illegally into Argentina where they were forced by gangsters

Bergoglio fought against the increasing number of casinos, such as the Central Casino in Mar del Plata above, in Buenos Aires.

to serve as prostitutes. Others were forced to work in garment factories, sewing clothing for eighteen hours a day and paid only one dollar per hour. If the women refused to put up with these working conditions, the factory owners took away their identification papers, and they could be shipped back home where there were no jobs. Many of these women eventually sought help from an organization called La Almeda, which publicized their plight and exposed the corrupt officials who allowed the factories to operate.

Cardinal Bergoglio also stepped in to publicize the exploitation of these women. In addition, he helped them escape the factories and prostitution rings by finding them places to live in convents run by Catholic nuns. Here they could begin to rebuild their lives removed from threats by the network of gangsters, politicians, and factory owners who had exploited them.[2]

The Church and the Government

In 2007, President Nestor Kirchner had decided not to run for reelection. Instead, he supported his wife—former Senator Cristina Kirchner—who was elected to replace him. Nevertheless, relations between the government and Cardinal Bergoglio had not improved. Although the economy was on the upswing, Bergoglio criticized the Kirchner administration for not doing more to help the poor—exemplified by the women he was trying to help escape exploitation.

Then, in 2010, the government proposed that gay couples should be permitted to marry. Bergoglio opposed this new proposal, believing that marriage had been defined for several thousand years as a union involving a man and a woman. However, he supported a compromise solution: so-called civil unions, or legal unions between two men or two women. These would be recognized by the government but would not involve church ceremonies. As leader of Argentina's Catholic bishops, he asked their support for this approach at a bishops' conference. They would not support him, however, because the Vatican opposed civil unions for gay couples.

As many in Argentina moved toward legalization of same-sex marriage, Bergoglio suggested civil unions as a compromise.

Later in 2010, the new law recognizing same-sex marriages was narrowly approved by Argentina's legislature—a majority believed that civil unions did not go far enough. The new law was approved over the strong opposition of the Catholic Church and Cardinal Bergoglio.

Leader of Interfaith Connections

While Bergoglio's relations with the Kirchner administration never improved, his interfaith connections grew year by year. Argentina had approximately one million Arab immigrants from the Middle East. In 2004, Bergoglio had become the first bishop to visit the Islamic Center of Argentina in Buenos Aires. Omar Abboud, who worked at the center, became a close friend of the cardinal. The two men met regularly and talked about a wide range of subjects, including music and religion.[3]

Argentina also had the largest Jewish population in Latin America. Over the years, Cardinal Bergoglio developed a close relationship with many Jewish leaders.

Bergoglio and the Dirty War

In 2010, a new accusation had arisen regarding the role of the Church and Cardinal Bergoglio during the Dirty War. As part of the military regime's campaign against their opponents, many young women had been arbitrarily arrested and thrown into prison. Some of these young women were pregnant. After they gave birth, their children were taken and given up for adoption. Afterward, many of the women were executed. The Mothers of the Plaza de Mayo—a group of women who had lost family members during the Dirty War—regularly held protests in the central square of Buenos Aires (the Plaza de Mayo). They claimed that the Church and Bergoglio knew about the adoptions.

Bergoglio denied these charges. The Mothers of the Plaza de Mayo had been co-founded by Esther Balestrino de Careaga, a Communist and close friend of Bergoglio's. When her daughter was arrested, Esther asked Bergoglio to hide the Communist pamphlets that she kept in her house. Bergoglio agreed, although he was opposed to Communism, and soon afterward Balestrino was also arrested and, as mentioned earlier, never seen again.[4]

Strengthening his interfaith connections, Bergoglio signs a joint declaration by Argentina's three main religions against terrorism.

Meanwhile, his long friendship with Rabbi Abraham Skorka grew even stronger. In 2010, Bergoglio, Skorka, and a protestant leader, Marcelo Figueroa, began a series of television programs in which they discussed the Bible and its teachings about various social issues, like sexuality and happiness. Skorka, who was rector of the Latin-American Seminary at Buenos Aires, received an honorary doctorate from the Catholic University in the capital, awarded by Cardinal Bergoglio.[5]

The following year, Bergoglio turned seventy-five. The Catholic Church required that at that age he must offer to resign as head of the Church in Argentina. What Cardinal Bergoglio could not have known was that Pope Benedict XVI would himself shortly resign from his position. And Bergoglio would become his successor, Pope Francis I.

Chapter 10

THE FIRST HUNDRED DAYS

Ever since the election of President Franklin Roosevelt in 1932, political analysts have looked at a president's first one hundred days for signs of how the new leader plans to govern. Roosevelt came to office in the depths of the Great Depression, when twenty-five percent of America's working population was unemployed. During the new president's first one hundred days in office, he proposed a wide range of new legislation designed to revive the economy and provide new jobs. Roosevelt also communicated a confidence in the future and his own ability to improve the nation that inspired Americans to have hope.

Papacy of the People

Other world leaders have been watched closely during their first three months in office, including Pope Francis, to determine their leadership style and their priorities. The first signals from the new pope suggested that he intended to follow the same course and live by the same values that had guided him as cardinal archbishop of Buenos Aires. Francis would be different from many of his predecessors—following a course marked by humility and creating a papacy of and for the people.

Instead of living in the Apostolic Palace—the home of other popes where 300 people served the Pontiff—he decided to live at the far humbler Casa Santa Maria, a place where priests visiting the Vatican stayed. For the formal ceremony installing him as the new pope, Francis invited the chief rabbi of Rome—the first time the rabbi had ever been asked to attend. It was an indication that this pope wanted to reach out as much as possible to other faiths, just as he had done in Buenos Aires.

Perhaps, most important, the new pope made it clear that bishops from across the world would have a much greater role in guiding the Church. This would not be a top-down papacy—where all decisions were made by the pope and the Papal Curia—but a "collegial" papacy where decisions would be made jointly by the pope and the Catholic bishops.

In addition, as Paul Vallely put it, "He set up a groundbreaking kitchen cabinet [small, informal cabinet] of eight cardinals from all around the world

In March 2013, Pope Francis moved into the papal apartment at the Vatican. This residence is far less grand than the Apostolic Palace.

to advise him on the running of the Church and the reform of the Vatican." They came to be known as the G8. Their role was to remake the Curia, which had not dealt effectively with the scandals involving priests molesting their young parishioners or the cover-up of these activities by bishops and cardinals. Among those appointed to the G8 were Cardinal Oscar Rodriguez Maradiaga, archbishop of Tegucigalpa in Honduras; Cardinal Reinhard Marx, archbishop of Munich; Cardinal Laurent Monswengo Pasinya, archbishop of Kinshasha, Democratic Republic of the Congo; Cardinal Oswald Gracias, archbishop of Bombay, India; and Cardinal Francisco Javier Errazuriz Ossa of Chile.[1]

Following the establishment of the new cabinet, priests and bishops from each region began communicating with the G8 about what changes they would like to see in the running of the Catholic Church. As one Catholic newspaper explained, "This move represents a highly significant rebalancing of forces within the government of the Catholic Church, and may pave the way for a form of representative Cabinet-type government instead of the model of an absolute monarchy that many believe has gone beyond the end of its useful life." But others were critical of the pope's move, saying it would lead toward the "demolition of the papacy." Yet another expert on the Church, Alberto Melloni, professor of the history of Christianity at the University of Modena, Italy, said it was the "most important step in the history of the church for the past 10 centuries."[2]

As proof of the respect he had gained around the world, leaders of many faiths were present at Pope Francis's inauguration.

Finally, in another act that symbolized change, Pope Francis—as part of a traditional Easter ritual—washed the feet of twelve prisoners at a juvenile prison. Two of them were women; no pope had ever washed the feet of women as part of the ritual before. And it immediately created controversy. Then he said to them: "This is a

The Great Communicator

Pope Francis has become unique as pope for his style of communication. He answers his own telephone and makes his own telephone calls in the Vatican. The pope also reached more than nine million people with his tweets to their phones. News writer John Freund explained that the pope's communication style was characterized by four characteristics:

First, he uses a simple, direct, colloquial language, a language that people today understand perfectly. Secondly he has a content that poses questions to people's consciences and hearts, responding to human suffering and the human yearning for inner seeking. . . . The third element is the way he gestures. Pope Francis does not only say certain things, he makes gestures that are able to convey this human richness. . . . Lastly he also knows how to spark the human imagination and sensitivity through recourse to figurative language. . . . Who could forget his appeal to priests and bishops to acquire the "smell of their sheep."[3]

symbol, a sign. Washing your feet means I am at your service. Help one another. This is what Jesus teaches us."[4]

In 2013, *Time* magazine named Pope Francis its Person of the Year. As the magazine put it, "He took the name of a humble saint and then called for a church of healing." As international editor, Bobby Ghosh, added: "He's changed perceptions of the church from being this out-of-touch institution to one that is humble and merciful. He changed the focus of the church from being focused on doctrine to becoming more about service."[5]

Change Was in the Air

As it turned out, the first one hundred days of the new papacy were only the beginning of what the pope had to say during the first year he was in office. In the past, the Catholic Church had not strongly supported the rights of gay people or welcomed them into the Catholic congregation. But on a trip to Brazil in September, Pope Francis told members of the press on his flight, "If someone is gay and searches for the Lord and has good will, who am I to judge gay people?"[6] It seemed to suggest that this pope had once again decided to reach out to a much broader group of the world's citizens. However, the pope gave no indication that he had changed his position on gay marriage. Later, he said, "Children mature seeing their father and mother [happy]. Their identity matures being confronted with the love their father and mother have, confronted with this difference."[7]

In October and November 2013, Pope Francis sounded themes that had characterized almost his entire

In a pre-Easter ritual symbolizing a willingness to serve others, Pope Francis washed the feet of inmates from a Roman prison in 2015.

priesthood. At a luncheon for the poor in the town of Assisi in Italy, where Saint Francis had lived, the pope said, "Many of you have been stripped by this savage world. [It] does not give employment, does not care if there are children dying of hunger."[8] In November, he spoke out against the "idolatry of money." The pope also emphasized once again his intention to change the top-down governing of the Catholic Church.[9]

Chapter 11

FRANCIS: THE PEOPLE'S POPE

I n his biography of the Pope Francis, author John Allen wrote:

In Argentina, both as a Jesuit and later as a bishop, Bergoglio generally dreaded the spotlight. On the rare occasions he did appear in high-profile situations, he had low-wattage appeal. He is described as "humble" and "shy" by those who liked him and "boring" and "gray" by those who didn't, and neither side would have labeled him charismatic. . . . Since becoming Pope, however, Bergoglio transformed into a beaming public figure. The pope's only surviving sibling, sixty-four year old Maria Elena Bergoglio, was asked in April 2013 what she made of the change, she jokingly said, "I don't recognize this guy!"[1]

In a public gesture of his love for all, Pope Francis blessed and hugged a man suffering from neurofibromatosis in 2013.

On the World's Stage

Throughout his career, Jorge Bergoglio had always seemed more comfortable in one-to-one conversations, whether he was talking to someone who lived in the slums, or one of his priests, or an important political leader. Now, suddenly, as pope, he found himself on the world stage. He appeared on magazine covers, he was widely interviewed, and his words were carefully monitored by the world press.

In 2014, Pope Francis delivered a powerful Lenten message. Lent is a period of prayer that lasts for several weeks before Easter Sunday. This is the day Christians believe Jesus Christ rose from the dead following his crucifixion. In his message to the world, Francis returned to old themes. "In imitation of the Master [Jesus Christ], we Christians are called to confront the poverty of our brothers and sisters, to touch it, to make it our own and to take practical steps to alleviate it."[2]

In March, US president Barack Obama met with Pope Francis in Rome. "Wonderful meeting you. I'm a great admirer," the president told him.[3] President Obama brought the pope a wooden chest filled with fruit and vegetable seeds from the White House garden. The wood came from the first Catholic cathedral in the United States, built in Baltimore.

However, the meeting with the President Obama did not stop Pope Francis a few months later from urging the United States to provide better treatment for children, unaccompanied by parents, illegally crossing over the border with Mexico. "I would like . . . to draw attention to the tens of thousands of children who migrate alone, unaccompanied, to escape poverty and violence," the pope said. "Many people forced to emigrate suffer, and often die tragically. Many of their rights are violated, they are obliged to separate from their families, and, unfortunately, continue to be the subject of racist . . . attitudes."[4]

A year earlier, the pope had visited Lampedusa, an Italian island, where he spoke with migrants from North Africa. Many had risked death to cross the Mediterranean Sea from North Africa to escape violence and poverty. At that time, the pope called upon the world to end the "global indifference" to their plight.[5]

This was part of the pope's continuing efforts to call attention to the plight of the world's poor and powerless—the same themes he had struck while serving as archbishop of Buenos Aires. For the Catholic Church to lead this struggle, Pope Francis believed that his church must reform itself. In his message at Christmas 2014, the pope warned that "a church that doesn't try to improve is like a sick body." He criticized the Papal Curia for believing "they are superior to others and not here for the service to others."[6]

A Bold Move

In 2015, Pope Francis announced the formation of a child abuse tribunal to deal with those bishops accused of covering up the abuses of Catholic priests. Approximately 850 priests had already been removed from their jobs,

In his short time as pope, Pope Francis has become incredibly popular as a pope of the people.

and 2,500 others had received penalties for their crimes. But no bishops had been held responsible because they "looked the other way" or moved a priest from one parish to another if he was accused of child abuse. The victims of this abuse had long asked for the Church to take action. But Pope Benedict and Pope John Paul II had refused to act.[7]

Encyclical on Climate Change

In June 2015, Pope Francis released a long-anticipated encyclical—report—on climate change. Francis was following in the footsteps of another Catholic leader, Pope Leo XIII, who in 1891 had called for the right of workers to unionize so they could achieve better working conditions—considered a revolutionary statement during that era. The encyclical by Pope Francis was called "Laudato Si," or "Praise be to You: On Care for Our Common Home."

In the 184-page encyclical, the pope wrote: "Climate change is a global problem with grave implications: environmental, social, economic, political and for the distribution of goods. It represents one of the principal challenges facing humanity in our day." The pope's encyclical supported the position of many environmental scientists who had been warning of the grave threat posed by climate change to the Earth. The pope added: "Our goal is not to amass information or to satisfy curiosity, but rather to become painfully aware, to dare to turn what is happening to the world into our

Pope Francis urges us all to take what we see in this information age and internalize it so that we may understand it as our own suffering.

own personal suffering and thus to discover what each of us can do about it."[8]

The pope went on to point out that climate change affects poor people most severely. They live in coastal areas where sea levels are rising and threatening to flood their homes. Their farms are located in rural areas of Africa that are stricken with drought. As a result, their poverty will only grow worse. The pope's message was applauded by many people, but criticized by others. Some Republicans in the United States, for example, suggested that the pope should stay out of politics. Other political leaders who question the evidence supporting climate change were also critical of the pope's encyclical.

Dr. Jim Yong Kim, president of the World Bank—an international lending institution—said, "Today's release of Pope Francis' first encyclical should serve as a stark reminder to all of us of the intrinsic link between climate change and poverty. As the effects of climate change worsen, we know that escaping poverty will become even more difficult."[9]

The Impact of World Leaders

World leaders have a unique opportunity to make a difference. They command the international stage, their statements draw the attention of the media, and their actions can change the lives of millions of people. As leader of the Roman Catholic Church, Jorge Bergoglio—Pope Francis I—not only has the ability to change the lives of Catholics whom he leads. But he can also impact the lives of many others by his words and his deeds.

So far, Pope Francis has been taking a leadership role in some of the most critical areas that afflict the world. But what he says and does have not marked a new direction for the man who served as a Jesuit, archbishop, and cardinal in Argentina. His values and priorities have remained remarkably consistent. As pope, these same values can now bring hope and change to the people of the world.

Chronology

1927—Jorge Bergoglio's grandparents emigrate from Italy to Argentina.

1930—The Great Depression begins.

1936—Jorge Mario Bergoglio is born in Buenos Aires.

1946—Juan Peron is elected president of Argentina.

1952—Evita Peron dies of cancer.

1956—Peron is overthrown by Argentina's military. Bergoglio enters a Catholic seminary to become a priest.

1958—Bergoglio enters a Jesuit Order.

1959—John XXIII becomes pope.

1960—Bergoglio enters Colegio Maximo to become a Jesuit.

1962—Vatican II begins in Rome.

1969—Bergoglio is ordained a Jesuit priest.

1971—Bergoglio is named novice master of Jesuits in Argentina.

1973—Peron is elected president of Argentina. Bergoglio becomes provincial of Jesuits in Argentina.

1974—Peron dies; Isabel Peron becomes president.

1976—Dirty War begins; thousands executed. Peron's government is overthrown; military rules Argentina.

1978—John Paul II becomes pope.

1979—Bergoglio becomes the rector of Colegio Maximo.

1982—Falklands War is fought between Argentina and Great Britain.

1983—Military government resigns; Raul Alfonsin is elected president.

1988—Carlos Menem is elected president of Argentina.

1992—Bergoglio becomes auxiliary bishop of Buenos Aires.

1998—Bergoglio becomes archbishop of Buenos Aires.

2000—Argentina is gripped by a severe economic crisis.

2001—Bergoglio is named cardinal.

2003—Nestor Kirchner becomes president of Argentina.

2005—Pope John Paul II dies; Benedict XVI becomes pope.

2007—Cristina Kirchner becomes president of Argentina.

2013—Pope Benedict resigns. Bergoglio is elected Pope Francis I.

2015—Pope Francis issues an encyclical on climate change, *Laudato Si*; he begins a tribunal to investigate bishops who covered up child abuse in the Church.

Chapter Notes

CHAPTER 1. ELECTION AS POPE

1. Austen Ivereigh, *The Great Reformer* (New York: Henry Holt, 2014), p. 350.
2. Ibid., pp. 357–358.
3. Ibid., p. 361.
4. Ibid., p. 363.
5. Ibid., p. 363.

CHAPTER 2. ITALIAN ROOTS

1. Sergio Rubin and Francesca Ambrogetti, *Pope Francis: Conversations with Jorge Bergoglio* (New York: G.P. Putnam's Sons, 2013), p. 5.
2. Austen Ivereigh, *The Great Reformer* (New York: Henry Holt, 2014), p. 13.
3. Ibid., p. 12.
4. Ibid., pp. 24–25.
5. Paul Vallely, *Pope Francis: Untying the Knots* (London, England: Bloomsbury Books, 2013), pp. 23–24.
6. Ivereigh, p. 32.
7. Rubin and Ambrogetti, p. 34.

CHAPTER 3. A YOUNG JESUIT

1. Austen Ivereigh, *The Great Reformer* (New York: Henry Holt, 2014), p. 66.
2. Ibid., pp. 66–79.
3. Paul Vallely, *Pope Francis: Untying the Knots* (London, England: Bloomsbury Books, 2013), p. 39.
4. Ivereigh, p. 94.
5. Ibid., pp. 94–95.

CHAPTER 4. CHAOS IN ARGENTINA

1. Austen Ivereigh, *The Great Reformer* (New York: Henry Holt, 2014), p. 110.
2. Jon Lee Anderson, "Pope Francis and the Dirty War," *The New Yorker*, March 14, 2013.
3. Sam Ferguson, "When Pope Francis Testified About the Dirty War," *New Republic*, March 14, 2013.
4. Ibid.
5. Ibid.
6. Austen Ivereigh, *The Great Reformer* (New York: Henry Holt, 2014), p. 138.

CHAPTER 5. IN THE CENTER OF CONFLICT

1. Elisabetta Piqué, *Pope Francis: Life and Revolution* (Chicago: Loyola Press, 2014), p. 85.
2. Ibid.
3. Ibid., p. 86.
4. Ibid.
5. Austen Ivereigh, *The Great Reformer* (New York: Henry Holt, 2014), pp. 178–179.
6. Ibid., p. 181.
7. Pique, p. 86.
8. Ibid., p. 88.
9. Kennedy Hickman, "The Falklands War: An Overview," About.com, http://militaryhistory.about.com/od/battleswars1900s/p/falklands.htm.
10. Ivereigh, pp. 203–205.

CHAPTER 6. ARCHBISHOP OF BUENOS AIRES

1. Evangelii Gaudium, http://w2.vatican.va/content/francesco/en/apost_exhortations/document
2. Elisabetta Pique, *Pope Francis: Life and Revolution* (Chicago: Loyola Press, 2014), p. 98.

3. Paul Vallely, *Pope Francis: Untying the Knots* (London, England: Bloomsbury Books, 2013), p. 101.
4. Ibid., p. 103.
5. Ibid., p. 104.
6. Ibid., pp. 104–105.
7. Ibid., p. 108
8. Ibid., p. 109.
9. Ibid., pp. 112, 109.
10. Pique, p. 101.

CHAPTER 7. CHURCH AND STATE IN CRISIS

1. Elisabetta Pique, *Pope Francis: Life and Revolution* (Chicago: Loyola Press, 2014), pp. 105–106.
2. Sergio Rubin and Francesca Ambrogetti, *Pope Francis: Conversations with Jorge Bergoglio* (New York: G.P. Putnam's Sons, 2013), pp. 130–131.
3. Ibid., pp. 142–143.

CHAPTER 8. A CARDINAL OF THE PEOPLE

1. Austen Ivereigh, *The Great Reformer* (New York: Henry Holt, 2014), p. 277.
2. Ibid., p. 282.
3. "Survivors: Pope Francis Saved Many in the Dirty Wars," *New York Times*, March 13, 2014.
4. Ibid.
5. Daniel Politi, "Argentinian Pastoral," *New York Times*, March 15, 2013.
6. Paul Vallely, *Pope Francis: Untying the Knots* (London, England: Bloomsbury Books, 2013), p. 129.
7. Ibid., p. 131.
8. Ibid., p. 132.
9. Ibid., p. 134.
10. Ibid., p. 137.

CHAPTER 9. FIGHTING CRIME AND CORRUPTION

1. Austen Ivereigh, *The Great Reformer* (New York: Henry Holt, 2014), pp. 307–309.
2. Ibid., pp. 328–331.
3. Ivereigh, p. 322.
4. "Survivors: Pope Francis Saved Many in the Dirty Wars," *New York Times*, March 13, 2014.
5. Ivereigh, p. 325.

CHAPTER 10. THE FIRST HUNDRED DAYS

1. Paul Vallely, *Pope Francis: Untying the Knots* (London, England: Bloomsbury Books, 2013), pp. 182–183.
2. Ibid., p. 184.
3. John Freund, "Pope Francis' Major Media Innovation," famvin, September 19, 2013, http://famvin.org/en/wo13/09/19/pope-francis-major-media-innovation.
4. Vallely, pp. 186–187.
5. Josh Levs and Michael Pearson, "Pope Francis Named Time Person of the Year 2013," CNN, December 11, 2013, http://www.cnn.com/2013/12/11/living/time-person-of-the-year/index.html.
6. "Pope Francis Returns from Trip to Brazil," World News, September 17, 2013, http://circanews.com/news/pope-francis-trip-to-brazil-2013.
7. "Pope Francis's Comments on Heterosexual Parenting Alienate Gay Catholics," Gay/Lesbian News, June 16, 2015, http://prideequalitypost.woodstitch.com/pope-franciss-comments-on-heterosexual-parenting.
8. "Pope Francis Urges Church to Focus on Helping Poor," BBC News, October 4, 2013, http://www.bbc.com/news/world-europe-24391800.

9. Zachary A. Goldfarb and Michelle Boorstein, "Pope Francis Denounces 'Trickle Down' Economic Theories in Sharp Criticism of Inequality," *Washington Post*, November 20, 2013, http://www.washingtonpost.com/ business/economy/pope-francis-denounces-trickle-down-economic-theories.

CHAPTER 11. FRANCIS: THE PEOPLE'S POPE

1. John L. Allen, *The Francis Miracle* (New York: Time Books, 2015), p. 4.
2. "Pope Francis' Lenten Message 2014," ZENIT, February 4, 2014, http://www.zenit.org/en/articles/ pope-francis-lenten-message-2014.
3. Michael Falcone and Mary Bruce, "President Obama Meets Pope Francis at the Vatican," ABC NEWS, March 27, 2014, http://abcnews.go.com/Politics/ president-obama-meets-pope-francis-vatican/ story?id=2307.
4. Josephine McKenna, "Pope Francis: End the 'Racist and Xenophobic' Approach to Migrants along U.S.-Mexico Border," Religion News Service, July 15, 2014, http://www.religionnews.com/2014/07/15/pope-francis-end-racist-xenophobic-approach-migrants-along-U.S.-Mexico-border.
5. Ibid.
6. Lucy Pawle and Susannah Cullinane, "Pope Francis Attacks 'Diseases' of Vatican in Curia Address," CNN, December 22, 2014, http://www.cnn.com/2014/12/22/ world/pope-francis-curia/index.html.
7. Elisabetta Povoledo and Laurie Goodstein, "Papal Tribunal to Try Bishops for Negligence," *New York Times*, June 11, 2015.

8. Laurie Goodstein, "In Footsteps of Popes Seeking Worldly Change," *New York Times*, June 19, 2015, A1, A6.
9. Coral Davenport, "Championing the Environment, Francis Takes Aim at Global Capitalism," *New York Times*, June 19, 2015, A8.

Glossary

barrio—Spanish term for slum neighborhood.

bishop—Church leader.

cardinal—Catholic Church leader who directs bishops and priests.

Casa Rosada—Pink House, home of the president of Argentina.

curia—Governing body of the Roman Catholic Church.

Dirty War—Execution of thousands in Argentina from the 1970s to the 1980s who were opposed to the government.

encyclical—A report from the pope.

Liberation Theology—Religious movement focused on freeing the poor from poverty.

Jesuit—Member of a Catholic religious order.

Jesuit provincial—Leader of the Jesuits in a specific geographic area.

Mass—Religious service in the Catholic Church.

novice—A young man learning to become a priest.

pope—Leader of the Roman Catholic Church.

seminary—School for training Catholic priests.

Vatican—Center of the Roman Catholic Church in Rome, Italy.

Further Reading

BOOKS

Ambrogetti, Francesca, and Rubin, Sergio. *Pope Francis: His Life in His Own Words*. New York: G.P. Putnam, 2013.

Ivereigh, Austen. *The Great Reformer*. New York: Henry Holt, 2014.

Pique, Elizabeth. *Pope Francis: Life and Revolution*. Chicago: Loyola Press, 2014.

Uschan, Michael. *Pope Francis*. Farmington Hills, MI: Lucent Books, 2015.

Vallely, Paul. *Pope Francis: Untying the Knots*. London, England: Bloomsbury, 2013.

WEBSITES

Catholic Online
http://www.catholic.org
The mission of Catholic Online (COL) is to accurately represent the Catholic religion, including its past and present.

The Holy See
http://w2.vatican.va/content/vatican/en.html
This site posts Pope Francis's speeches, meditations, and schedule.

MOVIES

Pope John Paul II. Directed by John Kent Harrison. 2005.

Saving Grace. Directed by Robert M. Young. 1986.

Index